TO THE U.S. STATE CAPITOL BUILDINGS

© 2024 by Jennifer Flanders
Prescott Publishing | Tyler, Texas
ISBN: 978-1-938945-46-5
www.flandersfamily.info

THIS BOOK BELONGS TO:

_____

name

IF FOUND, PLEASE CONTACT:

_____

phone number

_____

email

INTRODUCTION

This small passbook provides a perfect place to collect free, dated ink stamps from your visits to U.S. State Capitols.

Capitol buildings are filled with magnificent artwork, fascinating history, and many other unique and wonderful surprises, including an opportunity to hold $600,000 hard cash (in Little Rock, Arkansas) or to climb 296 steps to the top of the outer dome (in Topeka, Kansas) or to admire the incredible hand-stenciled walls and gorgeous mosaics and wander through voluminous libraries (in Des Moines, Iowa).

Every capitol building has a personality all its own just waiting to be discovered by the next generation of admirers. Best of all, they are all open to the public and are free to tour, so let's get started!

STATE CAPITOL CHECKLIST

- ☐ Alabama
- ☐ Alaska
- ☐ Arizona
- ☐ Arkansas
- ☐ California
- ☐ Colorado
- ☐ Connecticut
- ☐ Delaware
- ☐ Florida
- ☐ Georgia
- ☐ Hawaii
- ☐ Idaho
- ☐ Illinois
- ☐ Indiana
- ☐ Iowa
- ☐ Kansas
- ☐ Kentucky
- ☐ Louisiana
- ☐ Maine
- ☐ Maryland
- ☐ Massachusetts
- ☐ Michigan
- ☐ Minnesota
- ☐ Mississippi
- ☐ Missouri
- ☐ Montana
- ☐ Nebraska
- ☐ Nevada
- ☐ New Hampshire
- ☐ New Jersey
- ☐ New Mexico
- ☐ New York
- ☐ North Carolina
- ☐ North Dakota
- ☐ Ohio
- ☐ Oklahoma
- ☐ Oregon
- ☐ Pennsylvania
- ☐ Rhode Island
- ☐ South Carolina
- ☐ South Dakota
- ☐ Tennessee
- ☐ Texas
- ☐ Utah
- ☐ Vermont
- ☐ Virginia
- ☐ Washington State
- ☐ West Virginia
- ☐ Wisconsin
- ☐ Wyoming

WASHINGTON, DC

Capital city of the United States
seated in the District of Columbia
since 05/15/1880

Date visited: _____

Stamp:

ALABAMA

22nd state to join the union (12/14/1819)
Capital City: Montgomery, AL

Date visited: _____

Stamp:

ALASKA

49th state to join the union (01/03/1959)
Capital City: Juneau, AK

Date visited: _____
Stamp:

ARIZONA

48th state to join the union (02/14/1912)
Capital City: Phoenix, AZ

Date visited: _____

Stamp:

ARKANSAS

25th state to join the union (06/15/1836)
Capital City: Little Rock, AR

Date visited: _____

Stamp:

CALIFORNIA

31st state to join the union (09/09/1850)
Capital City: Sacramento, CA

Date visited: _____

Stamp:

COLORADO

38th state to join the union (08/01/1876)
Capital City: Denver, CO

Date visited: _____
Stamp:

CONNECTICUT

5th state to join the union (01/09/1788)
Capital City: Hartford, CT

Date visited: _____
Stamp:

DELAWARE

1st state to join the union (12/07/1787)
Capital City: Dover, DE

Date visited: _____

Stamp:

FLORIDA

27th state to join the union (03/03/1835)
Capital City: Tallahassee. FL

Date visited: _____
Stamp:

GEORGIA

4th state to join the union (01/02/1788)
Capital City: Atlanta, GA

Date visited: _____

Stamp:

HAWAII

50th state to join the union (08/21/1959)
Capital City: Honolulu, HI

Date visited: _____
Stamp:

IDAHO

43rd state to join the union (07/03/1890)
Capital City: Boise, ID

Date visited: _____

Stamp:

ILLINOIS

21st state to join the union (12/03/1818)
Capital City: Springfield, IL

Date visited: _____

Stamp:

INDIANA

19th state to join the union (12/11/1816)
Capital City: Indianapolis, IN

Date visited: _____

Stamp:

IOWA

29th state to join the union (12/28/1846)
Capital City: Des Moines, IA

Date visited: _____
Stamp:

KANSAS

34th state to join the union (01/29/1861)
Capital City: Topeka, KS

Date visited: _____
Stamp:

KENTUCKY

15th state to join the union (06/01/1792)
Capital City: Frankfort, KY

Date visited: _____

Stamp:

LOUISIANA

18th state to join the union (04/30/1812)
Capital City: Baton Rouge, LA

Date visited: _____

Stamp:

MAINE

23rd state to join the union (03/15/1820)
Capital City: Augusta, ME

Date visited: _____

Stamp:

MARYLAND

7th state to join the union (04/28/1788)
Capital City: Annapolis, MD

Date visited: _____

Stamp:

MASSACHUSETTS

6th state to join the union (02/06/1788)
Capital City: Boston, MA

Date visited: _____

Stamp:

MICHIGAN

26th state to join the union (01/26/1837)
Capital City: Lansing, MI

Date visited: _____

Stamp:

MINNESOTA

32nd state to join the union (05/11/1858)
Capital City: St. Paul, MN

Date visited: _____
Stamp:

MISSISSIPPI

20th state to join the union (12/10/1817)
Capital City: Jackson, MS

Date visited: _____
Stamp:

MISSOURI

24th state to join the union (08/10/1821)
Capital City: Jefferson City, MO

Date visited: _____
Stamp:

MONTANA

41st state to join the union (11/08/1889)
Capital City: Helena, MT

Date visited: _____

Stamp:

NEBRASKA

37th state to join the union (03/01/1867)
Capital City: Lincoln, NE

Date visited: _____

Stamp:

NEVADA

36th state to join the union (10/31/1864)
Capital City: Carson City, NV

Date visited: _____
Stamp:

NEW HAMPSHIRE

9th state to join the union (06/21/1788)
Capital City: Concord, NH

Date visited: _____

Stamp:

NEW JERSEY

3rd state to join the union (12/18/1787)
Capital City: Trenton, NJ

Date visited: _____
Stamp:

NEW MEXICO

47th state to join the union (01/06/1912)
Capital City: Sante Fe, NM

Date visited: _____

Stamp:

NEW YORK

11th state to join the union (06/26/1788)
Capital City: Albany, NY

Date visited: _____
Stamp:

NORTH CAROLINA

12th state to join the union (11/21/1789)
Capital City: Raleigh, NC

Date visited: _____

Stamp:

NORTH DAKOTA

39th state to join the union (11/02/1889)
Capital City: Bismark, ND

Date visited: _____

Stamp:

OHIO

17th state to join the union (03/01/1803)
Capital City: Columbus, OH

Date visited: _____

Stamp:

OKLAHOMA

46th state to join the union (11/16/1907)
Capital City: Oklahoma City, OK

Date visited: _____

Stamp:

OREGON

33rd state to join the union (02/14/1859)
Capital City: Salem, OR

Date visited: _____

Stamp:

PENNSYLVANIA

2nd state to join the union (12/12/1787)
Capital City: Harrisburg, PA

Date visited: _____

Stamp:

RHODE ISLAND

13th state to join the union (05/29/1790)
Capital City: Providence, RI

Date visited: _____

Stamp:

SOUTH CAROLINA

8th state to join the union (05/23/1788)
Capital City: Columbia, SC

Date visited: _____

Stamp:

SOUTH DAKOTA

40th state to join the union (11/02/1889)
Capital City: Pierre, SD

Date visited: _____

Stamp:

TENNESSEE

16th state to join the union (06/01/1796)
Capital City: Nashville, TN

Date visited: _____
Stamp:

TEXAS

28th state to join the union (12/29/1845)
Capital City: Austin, TX

Date visited: _____

Stamp:

UTAH

45th state to join the union (01/04/1896)
Capital City: Salt Lake City, UT

Date visited: _____

Stamp:

VERMONT

14th state to join the union (03/04/1791)
Capital City: Montpelier, VT

Date visited: _____

Stamp:

VIRGINIA

10th state to join the union (06/25/1788)
Capital City: Richard, VA

Date visited: _____
Stamp:

WASHINGTON STATE

42nd state to join the union (11/11/1889)
Capital City: Olympia, WA

Date visited: _____

Stamp:

WEST VIRGINIA

35th state to join the union (06/20/1863)
Capital City: Charleston, WV

Date visited: _____
Stamp:

WISCONSIN

30th state to join the union (05/29/1848)
Capital City: Madison, WI

Date visited: _____

Stamp:

WYOMING

44th state to join the union (04/10/1890)
Capital City: Cheyenne, WY

Date visited: _____
Stamp:

CAPITOL BUILDING
PHOTO ATTRIBUTIONS

US Capitol in Washington, DC - Martin Falbisoner. September 5, 2013. File: US Capitol and Grant Memorial.jpg.

Alabama - Josh Thompson from Fremont, CA. May 6, 2019. File: Alabama State House Men Working (48068674701).jpg.

Alaska - Jay Galvin from Pleasanton, CA. August 31, 2010. File: Alaska State Capitol Building.jpg.

Arizona - Wars. August 17, 2006. File: AZ State Capitol Building 80635.jpg.

Arkansas - Sharon Hahn Darlin. March 2, 2020. File: Little Rock, Arkansas (49611429692).jpg.

California - Tobias Haase from Hanover, Germany. October 4, 2005. File: Sacramento Capitol (23320659795).jpg.

Colorado - Jennifer Flanders from Tyler, TX. April 24, 2024. Personal photo.

Connecticut - jglazer75. June 17, 2005. File: Connecticut State Capitol, Hartford (cropped).jpg.

Delaware - Famartin. July 20, 2022. File: The east side of Delaware Legislative Hall (Delaware Capitol Building) in Dover, Kent County, Delaware.jpg.

Florida - DXR. July 11, 2016. File: Old Florida State Capitol, Tallahassee, East view 201607111.jpg.

Georgia - fw_gadget. August 11, 2009. File: Georgia State Capitol (3927365984).jpg.

Hawaii - w_lemay. May 12, 2022. File: Hawaii State Capitol, Beretania Street, Honolulu, HI - 52221221650.jpg.

Idaho - Tamanoeconomico. July 8, 2018. File: Idaho State Capitol, Boise.jpg.

Illinois - Teemu008 from Palatine, Illinois. May 19, 2012. File: Illinois State Capitol (7167050199).jpg.

Indiana - derivative work: Massimo Catarinella. September 29, 2008. File: StateCapitolIndiana.jpg

Iowa - Jennifer Flanders from Tyler, TX. May 25, 2023. Personal photo.

Kansas - Jennifer Flanders from Tyler, TX. May 26, 2023. Personal photo.

Kentucky - Peter Fitzgerald. March 27, 2007. File: Kentucky state capitol building.jpg.

Louisiana - Jim Plylar. January 10, 2010. File: Louisiana State Capitol 2.jpg.

Maine - Tony Webster from Minneapolis, Minnesota. October 15, 2016. File: Maine State Legislature Office (Capitol) - Augusta (30348592495).jpg

Maryland - Bestbudbrian. June 25, 2015. File: Thurgood Marshall statue and Maryland State House.jpg.

Massachusetts - Fcb981. September 29, 2007. File: Mass statehouse eb1.jpg.

Michigan - Phillip Hofmeister. Winter 2004/2005. File: Michigan-Capitol-2005.jpg.

Minnesota - Jonathunder. November 21, 2009. File: MinnesotaCapitol.jpg.

Mississippi - Tony Webster from Minneapolis, MN. June 20, 2016. File: State of Mississippi State Capitol (27565754440).jpg.

Missouri - Gina Strobel. July 15, 2017. File: Missouri State Capitol fountain view.jpg.

Montana - Martin Kraft. September 18, 2013. File: MK01799 Montana State Capitol.jpg.

Nebraska - Nanilluc. June 18, 2018. File: Nebraska State Capitol, Lincoln, NE.jpg.

Nevada - Amadscientist. January 19, 2012. File: Nevada State Capitol.jpg.

New Hampshire - AlexiusHoratius. December 6, 2012.
File: New Hampshire State House 6.jpg.

New Jersey - Lowlova. September 20, 2014. File: NJ
Capitol (cropped).jpg.

New Mexico - formulanone from Huntsville, USA.
May 17, 2017. File: NewMexicoStateCapitol-
SantaFe(36637491941).jpg.

New York - Shaunfrombrooklyn. September 2, 2017.
File: New York State Capitol building, full.jpg.

North Carolina - Farragutful. October 25, 2015. File:
2015 North Carolina State Capitol.jpg.

North Dakota - Bobak Ha'Eri. May 21, 2009. File:
2009-0521-ND-StateCapitol (cropped).jpg.

Ohio - Alexander Smith. May 8, 2004. File: Ohio
Statehouse columbus.jpg.

Oklahoma - Caleb Long. October 11, 2008. File:
Oklahoma State Capitol.jpg.

Oregon - Chalyptratus08. August 14, 2022. File: Oregon State Capitol 2022.jpg.

Pennsylvania - w_lemay. May 30, 2022. File: Pennsylvania State Capitol, Harrisburg, PA - 52441466369.jpg.

Rhode Island - Farragutful. December 18, 2019. File: 2019 Rhode Island State House 01.jpg.

South Carolina - Jennifer Flanders from Tyler, TX. July 26, 2022. Personal photo.

South Dakota - WeaponizingArchitecture. September 24, 2022. File: South Dakota State Capitol.jpg.

Tennessee - Peggy Anderson. September 4, 2014. File: Tennessee State Capitol in Nashville.jpg.

Texas - Daniel Mayer. November 2006. File: Texas State Capitol building-front oblique view.jpg.

Utah - GyozaDumpling. January 15, 2022. File: Utah State Capitol Building in 2022.jpg.

Vermont - Tom Holland. December 16, 2005. File: State House Vermont.jpg.

Virginia - Martin Falbisoner. September 7, 2013. File: Virginia State Capitol late morning.jpg.

Washington State - Joe Mabel. June 14, 2020. File: Washington State Capitol Legislative Building from Joel M. Pritchard Library 01.jpg.

West Virginia - F McGady. July 18, 2015. File: West Virginia Statehouse.jpg.

Wisconsin - Jennifer Flanders from Tyler, TX. May 17, 2023. Personal photo.

Wyoming - Jennifer Flanders from Tyler, TX. April 24, 2024. Personal photo.

Want a place to collect
National Park stamps,
as well?

PASSPORT
NATIONAL PARKS
UNITED STATES OF AMERICA
TO THE U.S.
NATIONAL
PARKS

Made in the USA
Coppell, TX
22 September 2024

37552147R20046